# Name That Animal Group!

By Kathleen Corrigan

**Published by The Child's World®**
800-599-READ • childsworld.com



**Photography Credits**
Jana Hake/Shutterstock.com, cover, title page, 21; Tetsuo Arada/Shutterstock.com, 5 (top); Howard Darby/Shutterstock.com, 5 (bottom); dibrova/Shutterstock.com, 7; Ewan Chesser/Shutterstock.com, 8-9, 29 (top left); Awei/Shutterstock.com, 11; Qasimphotographer/Shutterstock.com, 13; Tomas Kotouc/Shutterstock.com, 15 (top), 29 (top right); Sergey Uryadnikov/Shutterstock.com, 16-17, 30-31; Baolin/Shutterstock.com, 18-19; Milan Zygmunt/Shutterstock.com, 23; PhotopankPL/Shutterstock.com, 25; artmoods/Shutterstock.com, 27; AjayTVm/Shutterstock.com, 28; Ondrej Prosicky/Shutterstock.com, 29 (bottom left); Witsawat.S/Shutterstock.com, 29 (bottom right)

**ISBN Information**
9781503877948 (Reinforced Library Binding)
9781503878532 (Portable Document Format)
9781503879072 (Online Multi-user eBook)
9781503879614 (Electronic Publication)

**LCCN**
2025938214

Printed in the United States of America

## ABOUT THE AUTHOR

Kathleen Corrigan moved from elementary teaching to children's book writing to share wonder with young readers. Her adventures have taken her around the world —from tasting Moroccan street food to SCUBA diving Australia's Great Barrier Reef, searching for the Loch Ness Monster, and learning "thank you" in many languages (often amusing locals). With Antarctica and penguin encounters next on her list, she dreams of going to space and writing a book while there. Until then, she continues creating stories from every corner of Earth.

# Table of Contents



AS YOU READ, LOOK FOR

**COMMON SUFFIXES AND PREFIXES**

-er, -es, -est, -ful, -less, -ly, dis-, pre-, re-, un-

CHAPTER 1

# Amazing Animal Groups

Have you ever seen fish swimming together? Or birds flying with one another in the sky? Groups of animals have special names. When fish swim together, we call their group a school of fish.

Animal groups can have the funniest or strangest names. A group of lions is called a pride. A group of monkeys is a troop. These names make our talk more colorful and help us describe animals effectively.

In this book, you will find some of the most amazing names for animal groups. You will meet land animals that stand tall and ocean animals that swim endlessly. You'll also encounter birds with colorful wings and tiny bugs that work tirelessly as a team.

People have used these special names for years. Some names sound silly, but they are usually thoughtful. Many names help us see how animals act in the wild or how they look.

Get ready to be an animal group expert! Hopefully, you'll proudly share these wonderful words with your loved ones.

**DID YOU KNOW?**

**The names for groups of animals are called collective nouns. Many of the oldest names came from English hunters. They used special words to describe the animals they saw. A book published in 1486 had a long list of collective nouns.**

A school of fish
Many animals prefer to live in groups.
A pride of lions

# Land Animals

## A TOWER OF GIRAFFES

Look up, up, up! The tallest land animals on Earth stand together in a group called a tower of giraffes. What a perfect name! It is hard to disguise a group of giraffes!

Giraffes are one of the giants of the animal kingdom. The tallest giraffes can reach nearly 20 feet (over six meters) tall! Their necks alone can be six feet (almost two meters) long. This helps them reach the tastiest leaves at the tops of trees.

When giraffes walk together, they move gracefully. Their long legs step carefully as they travel endlessly across the **plains**. Baby giraffes learn to walk within an hour of being born.

A tower of giraffes has about 15 members. They protect each other by watching out for danger. Giraffes can see lions from far away. The tallest giraffe keeps lookout while the others eat peacefully.

Sadly, giraffes are becoming more uncommon. Humans remove trees so that the land can be used for something else. Fewer trees mean less food for these gentle giants. Thankfully, some people are working tirelessly to help prevent the loss of trees. This will help giraffes to live safely in the wild.

A tower of giraffes looks intently for food.

## A CRASH OF RHINOCEROSES

When rhinoceroses run together, the ground shakes. These powerful animals can run as fast as a car in the city. But rhinos are unable to see well. Some people say that is why a group of rhinos is called a crash. Rhinos might crash into things they cannot predict. Or maybe it is because they crash through the landscape.

Rhinoceroses are very strong and **robust**. Their tough, wrinkly skin is like armor. They look like prehistoric animals with their unusual horns and leathery skin.

Even with poor eyesight, rhinos can discover food and water in the wild. They use their amazing sense of smell to find water during the driest times of the year. Rhinos can smell water miles away!

Rhinos help other wildlife by reshaping their homes. As they eat plants, they spread seeds. Their heavy steps make paths that smaller animals can reuse to move around. By **disrupting** plants, rhinos help other animals.

Some people also call a group of rhinos a stubbornness. This name fits perfectly because rhinos often refuse to give up. Their power and size make them unstoppable when they decide to go somewhere!

They may look unfriendly, but rhinos are quite shy creatures. Rhinos are peaceful animals unless they are threatened.

A crash of rhinos grazes quietly.

## A PRICKLE OF PORCUPINES

What do you call a group of animals covered in sharp quills? A prickle of porcupines, of course!

Porcupines have up to 30,000 quills covering their bodies. These special hairs help keep them safe. When a porcupine feels unsafe, its quills stand up as a protective barrier. This makes it look bigger. Unlike what some people think, porcupines cannot shoot their quills. **Predators** must touch the porcupine to get pricked. The quills disconnect easily from the porcupine's skin. These quills have barbs on their ends which make them painful to remove. They get stuck in an animal's skin and cause a lot of discomfort.

Adult porcupines prefer to live alone. However, they sometimes form groups in the winter to help them keep warm. Porcupines spend most of the day sleeping in trees or dens. At night, they get restless and go out to find food. They eat bark, leaves, and berries. Then they return to their sleeping spot.

Baby porcupines are called porcupettes. They are born with soft quills that harden quickly. Mother porcupines protect their babies fearlessly. As porcupettes get bigger, they learn to climb trees and discover food on their own.

Porcupines are not unfriendly animals. They dislike fighting and prefer to be left alone. If you ever see a prickle of porcupines, watch them quietly from afar.

A prickle of porcupines has a new little porcupette.

**DID YOU KNOW?**
Porcupines are rodents, just like mice and squirrels. They are the second-largest rodents in North America. Only beavers are bigger.

## A SMACK OF JELLYFISH

Have you ever seen jellyfish floating in the ocean? A group of jellyfish is called a smack of jellyfish.

Jellyfish are unlike many other sea animals. They have no bones, brain, or heart. Their bodies are mostly water, and they feel like jelly. That is how they got their name!

Many jellyfish can glow in the dark. This special light is called **bioluminescence**. Jellyfish often use this unusual glow to defend themselves against predators. The bright, colorful flash of light can confuse animals that want to eat them.

Jellyfish have long, stringy arms called tentacles. These tentacles can sting. Some think the word "smack" describes the sudden, painful feeling you get from a tentacle's sting. While some stings feel like a small pinch, others are very painful. Lifeguards remind swimmers to stay away from jellyfish when a smack is floating by. You may be sorry if you disobey.

Jellyfish are some of the oldest animals on Earth. They have lived in the oceans for over 500 million years. Jellyfish were swimming in prehistoric seas before the dinosaurs walked on land!

A smack of jellyfish moves with the ocean and cannot swim against strong currents. They drift endlessly, floating where the water takes them. Jellyfish glide gracefully, like underwater umbrellas opening and closing.

A smack of jellyfish drifts calmly in the sea.

## A SHIVER OF SHARKS

When sharks swim together, they form a shiver of sharks! The word "shiver" might come from an old English word. It describes the way sharks move through water. Or maybe it is because sharks make us shiver with fear!

Sharks are some of the oldest animals in the world. Their prehistoric relatives swam in the seas over 400 million years ago. The biggest shark that ever lived was the megalodon. It could grow longer than a school bus!

Unlike what some people think, sharks are not mindless attackers. Most sharks are quite shy and prefer to avoid humans if possible. They are very careful hunters that help keep the oceans healthy.

Sharks have special senses that help them discover food. They have tiny, jelly-filled pores in their heads. These pores have **receptors** that sense electrical impulses. Some sharks can sense the electricity from a fish's beating heart!

The fastest sharks can swim as quickly as cars drive on a highway. Slower sharks move more restfully along the ocean floor searching for food.

Sadly, many sharks are disappearing from our oceans because people hunt them. Without sharks, the whole ocean ecosystem becomes unbalanced.

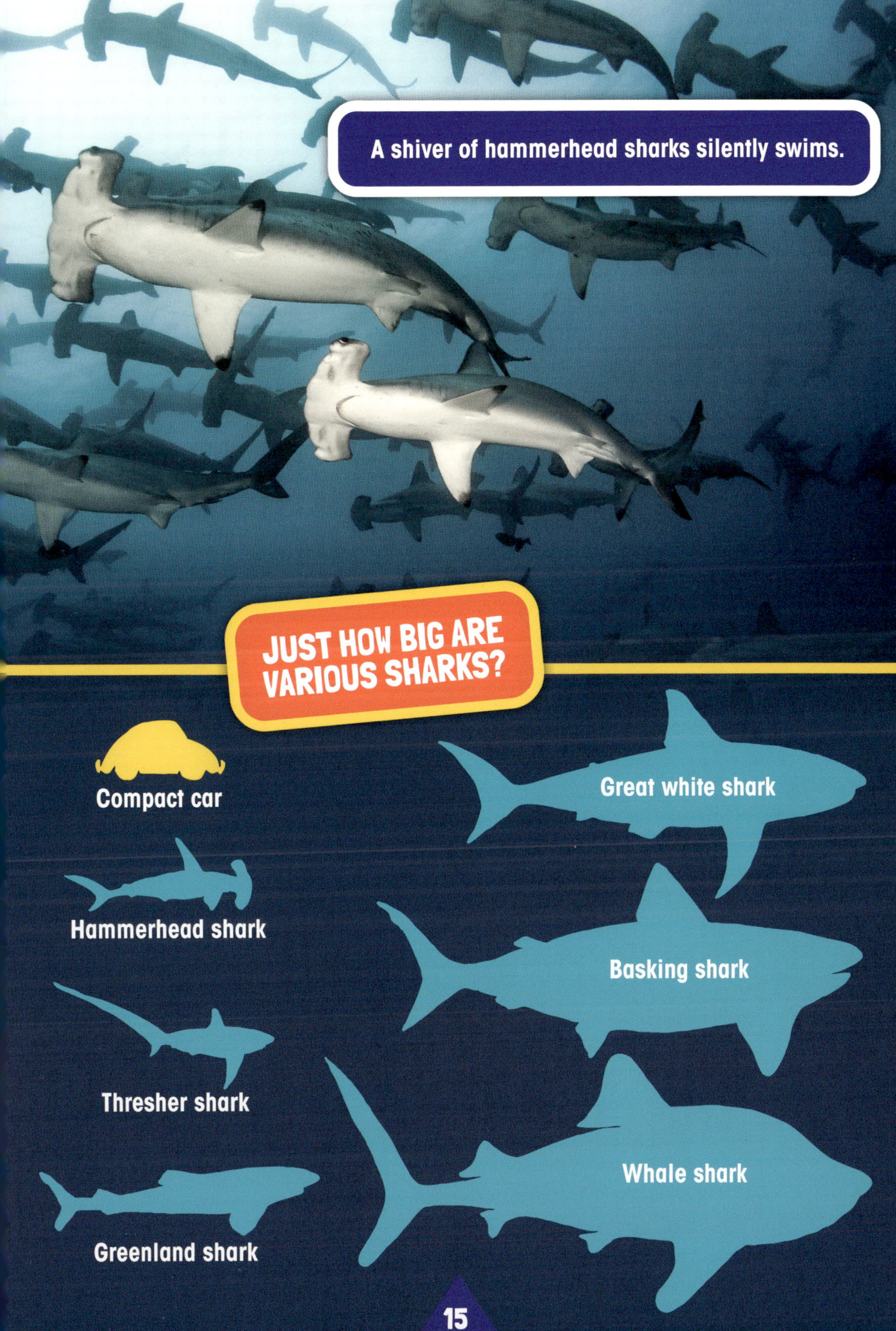
A shiver of hammerhead sharks silently swims.
JUST HOW BIG ARE VARIOUS SHARKS?
Compact car
Great white shark
Hammerhead shark
Basking shark
Thresher shark
Whale shark
Greenland shark

## A POD OF DOLPHINS

When dolphins swim together, they form a pod. A pod can have just a few dolphins or hundreds swimming playfully together.

Dolphins could be the smartest and friendliest animals in the ocean. They remember their friends for many years.

Dolphins talk to each other using clicks, buzzes, and whistles. They also use body movements to interact. Each dolphin has its own special whistle, like a name.

Dolphins are helpful hunters. They work together to catch fish by swimming circles around them to corner them. Mother dolphins teach their babies hunting tricks. Their hunches about where to find food are usually right!

**DID YOU KNOW?**

Dolphins can recognize themselves in mirrors. Scientists put a small mark on a dolphin and show it a mirror. The dolphin will look carefully at the mark on their skin. This shows that dolphins recognize themselves in their reflections. Very few animals can do this.

Dolphins seem like joyful animals. They often ride waves and jump out of the water. Dolphins seem to enjoy playing endlessly, just like we do.

Unlike fish, dolphins must come to the surface for air. They take a quick breath and then disappear underwater again.

Dolphins might be very thoughtful animals. Some people have reported dolphins helping hurt swimmers by gently pushing them to the surface. Other people have said that braver dolphins have prevented sharks from attacking humans. But we don't know these things for sure.

A large pod of dolphins swims joyfully together.

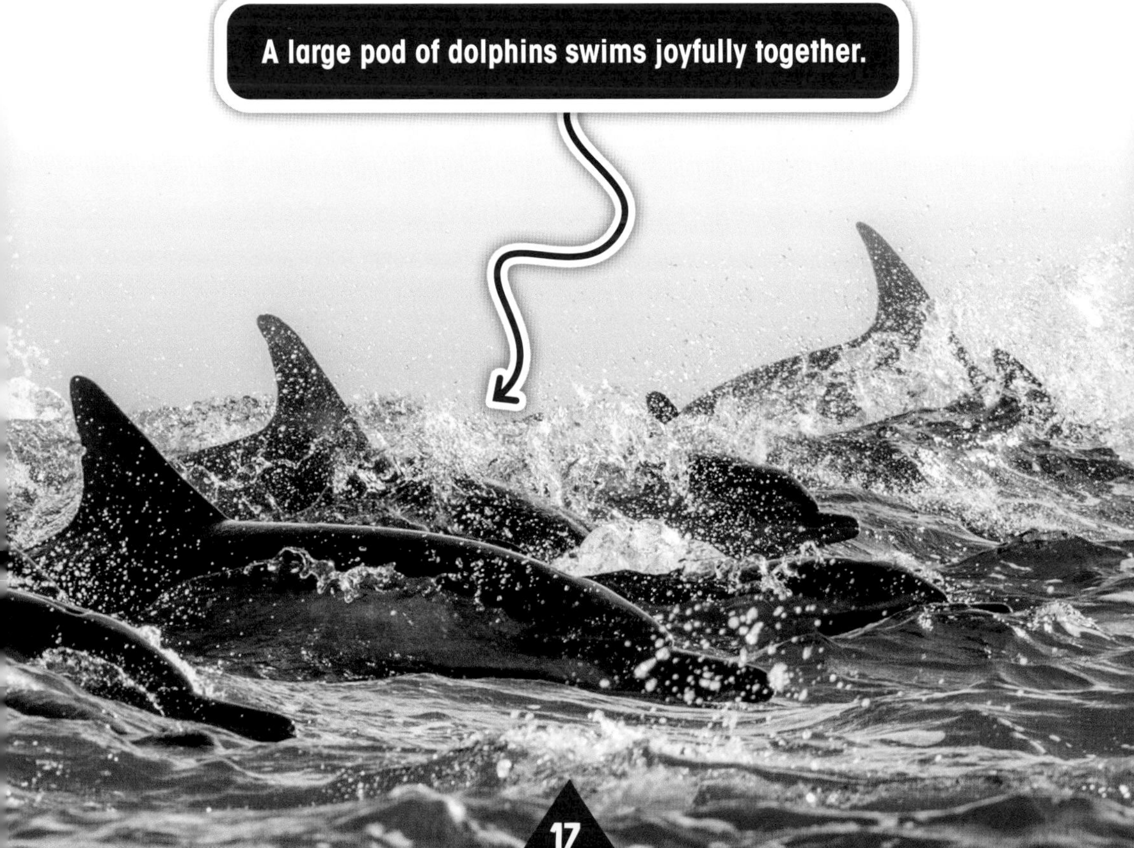

CHAPTER 4

# Birds of a Feather

## A QUARREL OF SPARROWS

Have you ever heard little birds chirping loudly at each other in trees or bushes? Those might be sparrows! A group of sparrows is called a quarrel. It's a perfect name for them. These tiny birds make the noisiest chirps and buzzes when they gather.

Sparrows are restless birds. They hop quickly from place to place, searching tirelessly for food. Sparrows really enjoy eating grains and seeds. They also grab small meals such as flies, ants, and tiny moths. Sparrows even eat the bugs squished on the front of cars or from a spider's web!

Sparrows may be smaller than some birds, but they are not boring. When sparrows gather in large groups, they make a lot of noise. In fact, it sounds like they are disagreeing with each other! This is why we call them a quarrel. Their cheerful songs and endless energy make gardens livelier. Plus, they eat many unwanted bugs, which is a huge bonus.

Sparrows prepare to lay their eggs by building a safe nest. They will carefully rebuild the nest if it gets damaged or destroyed by wind or rain.

These sparrows are having fun busily flying on a hot day.

## DID YOU KNOW?

House sparrows can reproduce very quickly. A single pair might have over 20 babies in just one year! That's a lot of sparrows to join the quarrel!

## A FLAMBOYANCE OF FLAMINGOS

When flamingos gather, they are known as a flamboyance. With their bright pink feathers, they certainly are flamboyant! Do you know the saying "birds of a feather flock together"? Flamingos are a perfect example of this phrase. These colorful birds often stand on one leg!

Flamingos are easy to spot with their long necks, curved bills, and pink feathers. It might surprise you, but flamingos aren't born pink. They start out white or gray. Their diet of tiny shrimp and **algae** slowly turns them pink. The healthiest flamingos have pinker feathers than others!

In the wild, flamingos are never friendless. They dislike being alone and live in huge groups. Some flamboyances have thousands of birds! They rebuild their mud nests every year. Most flamingos stay with the same partner for many years. The whole flamboyance works together to protect the young birds. They keep the smaller chicks together to prevent attacks from predators.

Flamingos have a very unusual way of eating. They turn their heads upside down and dip their bills into the water. Inside their bills are comb-like edges that filter out the tastiest animals and plants.

Flamingos make special honks and hisses to communicate with one another. When these wonderful birds fly together, they create one of nature's prettiest sights!

Flamingos live in shallow lakes and marshes.

## A CHARM OF HUMMINGBIRDS

A group of hummingbirds is called a charm. Hummingbird charms are usually small, just like the birds themselves. It is rare to see many hummingbirds together. These tiny birds move so quickly they seem to disappear and reappear like magic. Their colorful feathers shine brightly in the sunlight with blues, greens, and reds. Meanwhile, their tireless wings beat so fast they make a humming sound. So hence their name.

Hummingbirds are the smallest birds in the world. But don't think they are helpless! They are fearless. Hummingbirds dislike other birds near their flowers. They will boldly chase away bigger birds and other hummingbirds.

Hummingbirds can do amazing things. They can fly backward and even stay still in the air! Hummingbirds are restless during the day, visiting countless flowers. Typically, at night, hummingbirds may enter a deep sleep called **torpor**. During torpor, their heartbeat slows down to save energy. They often do this when the weather is colder, too.

These wonderful birds help flowers grow. They use their long bills to reach deep into blossoms. As they drink nectar, they unintentionally carry pollen between different flowers. Many bushes and trees would be fruitless without these tiny **pollinators**. When these busy birds zoom between flowers, they make the garden come alive!

# A HUMMINGBIRD'S BUSY DAY

## NIGHT

**RESTFUL SLEEP**

May enter torpor to save energy

## DAWN

**WAKING UP**

Heart rate increases from 50 to 1,200 beats per minute

A hummingbird can visit 1,500+ flowers in a day!

## MORNING

**BREAKFAST TIME**

Visits 500+ flowers before noon

## MIDDAY

**DEFENDER**

Fearlessly protects feeding area

## AFTERNOON

**BUSY POLLINATOR**

Visits another 700+ flowers

## EVENING

**FINAL FEEDING**

Visits 300+ flowers before sunset

CHAPTER 5

# Tiny But Mighty

## A COLONY OF TERMITES

Have you ever seen a giant mound of dirt rising from the ground like a tiny skyscraper? That might be home to a colony of termites! These insects work together to build their amazing homes.

Not all termites live in huge mounds. Many termites make their homes inside dead trees. Others make their homes underground or even inside wooden houses. No matter where they live, termites are tireless workers. They dig countless tunnels and rooms. Some termite mounds in Africa are taller than your house! The insects carefully rebuild any broken parts of their homes. They help each other and never stop working.

Termites may look like ants, but they are more closely related to cockroaches. However, unlike most cockroaches, termites have special jobs in their colony. Some are workers who find food and build the nest. Others are fearless soldiers who protect everyone. Each colony also has a king and queen who remain underground. The queen termite is the most important and powerful. She can lay thousands of eggs every day!

Termites may seem unhelpful when they eat wooden houses. In nature, however, they do an important job. They break down dead trees and other plant material. This recycles the plants back into soil. Without termites, forests would be full of fallen trees that never disappear.

## DID YOU KNOW?

In some places, people eat termites. They are full of protein and can be roasted or fried for a crunchy snack. In parts of Africa and Asia, termites and their mounds are used to make medicine.

This termite mound is larger than a person.

## A LOVELINESS OF LADYBUGS

Sometimes bright red beetles with black spots gather on leaves and flowers. This is referred to as a loveliness of ladybugs. This wonderful name fits these insects well because they are lovely to look at.

Ladybugs are hungrier than most insects. Bugs called aphids harm plants. But one ladybug eats more than 50 aphids a day! Gardeners are thankful when these colorful beetles visit their plants.

Ladybugs are eaten by other insects. But they are not helpless. They can release a yellow fluid that works like a **repellent** to predators. Ladybugs can also tuck in their legs and pretend to be lifeless. Additionally, their bright colors can sometimes scare away predators.

The life of a ladybug is full of change. They start as tiny eggs that hatch into larvae that look unlike adult ladybugs. These larvae look like tiny alligators, and they are even hungrier than grown ladybugs. Next is the **pupa** stage, when they rebuild themselves from a larva into an adult. As adults, they become the spotted beetles we recognize.

Ladybugs seem to disappear in winter. But they don't really vanish. When fall comes, ladybugs hide in tree bark, cracks, or even inside houses. Often a loveliness of ladybugs will gather in one place to keep warm. Hundreds of ladybugs may huddle together until they reappear in spring.

A small loveliness of ladybugs prepares to disappear for the winter.

## A CLUTTER OF SPIDERS

Most spiders like to live alone and even eat other spiders. Some kinds of spiders gather in groups, though. They form a clutter of spiders.

Spiders are among the fastest hunters in the insect world. They catch many pests in their sticky traps. A hungry spider can eat hundreds of bugs, including mosquitoes. Many of us think spiders are scary. But most spiders are harmless to humans,

Spiders spin fine webs. The silk comes from special spinnerets (openings) on their bodies. This silk starts as a liquid protein but hardens in air. When breezes break their webs, spiders can rebuild them. Some of the busiest spiders remake their webs daily.

Not all spiders spin webs. Some chase and grab their prey. Others hide until an insect passes by. There are countless types of spiders in almost all habitats on Earth.

A clutter of baby spiders rests quietly on their mother's web.

## DELIGHTFUL ANIMAL GROUPS

We have learned about many wonderful animal groups in this book. From a tower of giraffes to a loveliness of ladybugs, animals gather for many reasons. Some are safer together. Others find food more easily in groups than on their own.

The special names for animal groups help us remember how amazing each one is. A crash of rhinoceroses sounds wildly powerful. A charm of hummingbirds sounds magical. These colorful names make learning about animals both fun and exciting!

So, next time you see a group of animals together, find out if they have a special name. One day, you might see a labor of moles, a graze of raccoons, or a mischief of rats. You might spot a quarrel of sparrows or a clutter of spiders. These wonderful creatures share our world. It can be a joy to learn more about them.

# COMMON SUFFIX AND PREFIX WORD LISTS

**-er**
attackers
bigger
braver
colder
eaters
fewer
gardeners
hungrier
hunters
larger
livelier
longer
pinker
safer
slower
smaller
stinger
swimmers
taller
workers

**-es**
bushes
buzzes
cockroaches
hisses
hunches
illnesses
marshes
mosquitoes
passes
patches
rhinoceroses
touches

**-est**
biggest
busiest
driest
fastest
friendliest
funniest
healthiest
largest
noisiest
oldest
prettiest
quickest
smallest
smartest
strangest
tallest
tastiest

**-ful**
careful(ly)
cheerful
colorful
delightful
graceful(ly)
hopeful(ly)
joyful(ly)
painful
peaceful(ly)
playful(ly)
powerful
restful(ly)
thankful(ly)
thoughtful
(un)helpful
wonderful

**-less**
countless
endless(ly)
fearless(ly)
friendless
fruitless
harmless
helpless
lifeless
mindless
restless
tireless(ly)

**-ly**
additionally
boldly
brightly
busily
calmly
carefully
certainly
closely
easily
effectively
endlessly
fearlessly
gently
gracefully
hopefully
intently
joyfully
loudly
lovely
mostly
nearly
peacefully
perfectly
playfully
proudly
quickly
quietly
really
restfully
sadly
safely
silently
slowly
thankfully
tirelessly
typically
unfriendly
unintentionally
usually
wildly
wrinkly

**dis-**
disagreeing
disappear(ing)
discomfort
disconnect
discover
disguise
dislike
disobey
disrupting

**pre-**
predators
predict
prefer
prehistoric
prepare(s)
pretend
prevent(ed)

**re-**
reappear
rebuild
receptors
recognize
recycles
referred
reflection
refuse
related
release
remain
remake
remember
remind
remove
repellent
reports
reproduce
reshaping
return
reuse

**un-**
unable
unbalanced
uncommon
underground
underwater
unfriendly
unhelpful
unintentionally
unless
unlike
unsafe
unstoppable
until
unusual
unwanted

# GLOSSARY

**algae (AL-jee):** small plants without roots or stems that grow in water or on damp surfaces

**bioluminescence (by-oh-loo-mih-NESS-enss):** light made by a living organism

**disrupting (dis-RUP-ting):** disturbing and messing up

**plains (PLAYNZ):** large areas of mostly flat land

**pollinators (POLL-uh-nay-turz):** living things that carry pollen grain to a plant so a seed may be fertilized

**predators (PRED-uh-turz):** wild animals that hunt other animals for food

**pupa (PYOO-puh):** the stage when a larva changes to an adult insect

**receptors (reh-SEP-turz):** body structures that receive sensory information

**repellent (reh-PEL-unt):** a substance that drives something away

**robust (roh-BUST):** strong and healthy

**torpor (TOR-pur):** a paused state of physical or mental inactivity in an animal

# INDEX